Dinosaurs

Chapter 6
Lesson 96: Reversed Vowels
Lexile® Measure: 600L

Printed in the United States of America

Copyright © September 2012 by Reading Horizons

No part of this publication may be reproduced, stored in a retrieval system, or transmitted in any form or by any means, electronic, mechanical, photocopying, recording, or otherwise, without the prior permission of the copyright owner.

ISBN 978-1-62382-050-3

Millions of years ago, dinosaurs walked on the Earth. They lived in many different places. They lived on open plains. They lived in forests. They lived in swamps and lakes. They even lived in the ocean.

Some scientists say that dinosaurs were actually reptiles. Others say they are closely related to birds. Either way, most dinosaurs were usually hatched from eggs. Some dinosaurs were giant sized. Some dinosaurs were medium sized. Other dinosaurs were as small as chickens.

Dinosaurs were covered with strong, scaly skin. Visually, their skin looked like armor. Some dinosaurs even had hard plates or spikes. Most had small craniums. They were not very brilliant.

The dinosaurs lived during three ages of time. These time periods were called Triassic, Jurassic, and Cretaceous.

Dinosaurs that lived during the Triassic period include Coelophysis, Plateosaurus, and Camposaurus. Crocodiles and turtles also lived during that time.

Names of dinosaurs from the Jurassic period seem more familiar. The Stegosaurus, Allosaurus, and Brachiosaurus all lived in the Jurassic period.

The Cretaceous period was virtually the last for the dinosaurs. The most famous dinosaurs during this time were the Tyrannosaurus Rex, Ankylosaurus, Triceratops, and Velociraptor.

Mysteriously, dinosaurs became extinct sometime after the Cretaceous period. Maybe they died all at once. Maybe they gradually disappeared. No one really knows. One possible theory is that a giant meteor crashed into the Earth and destroyed them.

Some scientists and historians suggest that there were other forms of chaos. Such forms of chaos include extreme volcanic eruptions and biological changes. Bacteria and disease could have caused them to die. It remains a mystery.

It may be another millennium before we know the actual cause of the dinosaurs' extinction. Maybe we'll never know.

The End

Comprehension Questions

1. What is one thing that this passage tells you about dinosaurs?

    a. what they ate

    b. when they lived

    c. how each dinosaur got its name

2. When did dinosaurs live on the Earth?

    a. last year

    b. yesterday

    c. millions of years ago

3. Which of the following groups of animals is NOT *extinct*?

    a. cats

    b. dinosaurs

    c. saber tooth tiger

4. Which of the following is NOT a likely cause of dinosaur extinction?
    a. They ran out of food to eat.
    b. Too many people hunted them.
    c. A meteor hit the Earth and killed all of the dinosaurs.

5. Which is a good example of *chaos*?
    a. a messy room
    b. crayons that are neatly organized in a box
    c. a classroom of students who are listening to their teacher

Skill Words

actual	familiar	mysteriously
actually	giant	period
bacteria	gradually	periods
biological	historians	Plateosaurus
Brachiosaurus	medium	Triassic
brilliant	meteor	usually
chaos	millennium	virtually
craniums	millions	visually

Most Common Words

a	have	open	walked
after	in	or	was
all	into	other	way
also	is	others	we
and	it	places	were
another	know	say	with
are	knows	seem	years
as	last	small	
at	like	some	
be	lived	such	
before	looked	that	
called	many	the	
closely	more	their	
could	most	them	
different	names	there	
earth	never	these	
even	no	they	
for	not	this	
forms	of	three	
from	on	time	
had	once	to	
hard	one	very	

Challenge Words

Cretaceous	ocean	theory
either	scientists	